Deano The Dinosaur

For Jaxon, Mason, and everyone who likes to stomp and roar like a dinosaur! - Linda

Written by Linda Rigby
Illustrated by Tanaya Lahrs

ROA

Deano the dinosaur
bellows with a roar.

He's woken up hungry and
his tummy's feeling sore.

Deano jumps up out of
bed and calls to his mum,

'I'm hungry for breakfast —
I can't wait to fill my tum!'

She makes him breakfast but
he needs a lot more,

And they don't have time to
go to the dinosaur store.

SOY

Lucky for them, they don't
even have to leave home.

They have a veggie garden
where lots of food is grown.

Deano stomps down the path
towards the veggie patch.

He gets to the little gate and
opens up the latch.

Straight away, Deano picks snow
peas and green beans,

And pops them in his mouth
because he loves crunchy greens.

Just behind the corn, he sees some rainbow chard.

Then finds pumpkin and leek
without looking very hard.

Deano looks for carrots,
potatoes and swedes,

He pulls them up carefully
and dodges all the weeds.

Nearly done as he picks
the broccolini.

Then he remembers to go
back for some zucchini.

SOY

He gives them to mum,
who has a clever plan.

She adds a few nice sauces
and cooks them in a pan.

He gobbles it all up and
feels his full tummy.

Deano thanks his mum and tells her,
'That was so YUM-MY!'

ENCOURAGING CHILDREN TO EAT VEGETABLES

Well balanced nutrition includes a variety of food groups, but vegetables are usually the hardest for us to learn to like. So, follow the tips below... and allow time. Children set their own pace.

The good news is you have already made a start! Reading picture books about vegetables and incorporating the foods into play are some of the best ways to familiarize your child with vegetables, so they are more likely to explore, taste and learn to enjoy eating them.

Food play is a gentle way for children to explore vegetables without pressure. Try inviting your little dino to touch, smell or sort veggies before they appear on the plate. Stack cucumber 'dino scales,' line up peas as tiny 'dinosaur eggs,' or crunch carrot sticks like 'jungle branches.'

Pretend broccoli is a 'mini forest' for dinosaurs to stomp through, sniff or carry. These small, imaginative moments help children feel safe, curious and connected — building comfort long before tasting is expected. Play makes food fun, and fun helps little dinos feel brave.

When Deano wakes up hungry — with a big dino ROAR — he's ready to chomp his way into the day. Hunger is a great time for little explorers to discover that nutritious foods can satisfy their tummy, which is great reinforcement for them to eat more. Adding a few veggies to breakfast, or popping fruit or vegetables into meals and snacks, helps make them feel like a normal, everyday part of eating. These tiny, playful moments of exposure build comfort and confidence, helping children learn that nutritious foods can be both satisfying and fun to explore.

Model good balanced nutrition. Let your child see you eating, and enjoying, a variety of fresh foods especially a wide range of vegetables.

Pressuring or punishing children at mealtimes results in them having a negative association with foods, and the stress can ruin their appetite. Set up mealtimes to be relaxing and enjoyable. Relaxation is not only better for digestion, using mealtimes as an opportunity to enjoy each other's company together builds strong family connections.

Serve a wide variety of vegetables and highlight their sensory qualities in positive, playful ways. Starting early helps young children build familiarity and gives them the best chance of learning to enjoy vegetables over time.

Shhh! Don't mention it's healthy. 'Healthy' is not a good motivator for children to eat, instead be encouraging! Speak about vegetables in a positive manner using rich sensory descriptions.

Lastly, take the pressure off yourself by understanding it is not a parents' job to make children eat, only to offer nutritional foods in a positive manner and allow children to learn to enjoy eating a variety of foods at their own pace.

While using these ideas will work for many families, there will be others who need more specialized help. A small percentage of children experience significant difficulty accepting new foods, and children with disability, delays, and neurodiversity are more likely to be among them. If you are concerned, reach out to a health professional who can provide more personalized help.

For further information, visit www.stellarchilddevelopment.com.au

Published by Stellar Child Development.

Stellar Child Development acknowledges the traditional owners of the lands upon which this book was created, bunurong/boon wurrung country of the kulin nation and awabakal country of the awabakal nation. We recognise their storytelling history, and continuing connection to the land, sea and culture. We pay our respects to elders past and present.

Design and Illustration by Tanaya Lahrs at Arttay Designs
www.arttaydesigns.com.au

ISBN
Hardcover: 978-1-923203-06-8   Paperback: 978-1-923203-07-5

First published 2026

A catalogue record for this book is available from the National Library of Australia

Other titles:

| Ten Hungry Carrots | Lulu's Rainbow Feast | Lulu's Activity Book |

My heartfelt thanks to Rod and Jake for your constant love and support, to Tanaya for your generous expertise and kindness, and to my PWC Scribe Tribe for all the creative vibes.

Please check www.stellarchilddevelopment.com.au